GW01393145

Prop

PETER JAEGER was born in Montreal, Canada. He has taught writing and theory at Dartington College of Arts, Royal Holloway, University of London. He currently teaches Creative Writing at Roehampton University. His previous publications include *Power Lawn* (1999), *ABC of Reading TRG* (1999), and *Eckhart Cars* (Salt Publishing, 2004). He lives in London and Somerset.

Also by Peter Jaeger

Power Lawn (1999)
ABC of Reading TRG (1999)
Eckhart Cars (2004)

Prop

PETER JAEGER

SALT

CAMBRIDGE

PUBLISHED BY SALT PUBLISHING
PO Box 937, Great Wilbraham, Cambridge CB21 5JX United Kingdom

Salt Publishing 2007
Printed and bound in the United Kingdom by
Biddles Ltd, King's Lynn, Norfolk

Typeset in Swift 9.5 / 13

ISBN 978 1 84471 324 0 hardback

Salt Publishing Ltd gratefully acknowledges
the financial assistance of Arts Council England

ARTS COUNCIL
ENGLAND

1 3 5 7 9 8 6 4 2

for Zoë

Contents

Acknowledgements

Many thanks to Tim Atkins, Caroline Bergvall, Ken Brake, Rajiv and Swati Chanchani, John Gaynor, Steve Gould, Chris and Jen Hamilton-Emery, Keith Hartman, Jeff Hilson, Zoë Hope, Kaz, Alaric Newcombe, Earl Stefanyshen, Fred Wah. Some of these poems appeared in an earlier form in *onedit* (http://www.onedit.net/index2.html)— thanks also to the editor. Thanks to Andrea Brady for including readings from a selection of these poems at *Archive of the Now* (http://people.brunel.ac.uk/~enstaab2).

"When you investigate the work of the sternum thoroughly, this is the work of the sternum."

EDMOND EIHEI

probably used
for rain, greener

waterfalls &
some description:

orange stamen,
bones & spacious

calcite seeming
less than pebbled

pebbled everywhere—
not a stone in sight

winter rain on the prong
of the ridge, on the mud

will be mud up high, it
will be pelted mud so

colder the hood hail
pelts—this is a hail

from up high's past
whenever the clouds

will be, will be clouds &
even the snow

will be snow that shedding
stuff she said it equals

lakes submerge us
in our strength of cool

soft ribboned hues
the brightest outlines

closer to the lakes
hulled by silt &

grass banks, rust
pumping pine

lengthens a granite
alignment

scattered on charity,
so cool the lake

expanding limbs
your broadened foot

& toes extend, always
to an upper clear

a brighter line
from fathoms

warm head pointing
east, pointing at migrant

pearls—where eyes meet
river, river bends to

mist, where stones meet
pale, pale whitens

swelled down from hills,
quick grids of snow

& further up right up
to shoulders with temples

trees tuned to winter, know
what should be known & snow

for toes & teeth of rice,
a smell or taste of wind

in the throat, sweeping
the road's edge, temple

roof gripped by frost the
trickling stream or 50 yen

how autumn
values spring

supporting your plan—
how leaves claim

the garden's edge
isn't edge,

how you show this
far from home

it stems from what is *is*
into air it's inside too

& pores are eyes
they open up the skin

remaining clear
they see you breathing

lasered out of rock &
tungsten hot

the quarter moon a rind
still held by morning heat
too high already in the sun

a white-cheeked bird with
crested skull without a name
without the name of the bird

she glides down from the curry bush
what kind it's just called
curry bush her fingers pluck

& crush those silver leaves
the moon still peeling overhead

so wet the skin wet the cold
round foot elbow turns

up to the waters spread apart
wet the quick push quick

word & numbers dates in a push
underfoot, unseen, they push

at the wet an equal exit
& we leave there soaking

in a simple, smallish pond,
a smaller stream, soaking

up a list where limbs
stay each afloat

waiting in the heat
for home

is where the heart
is maybe where

the job is maybe
mindful of the rise

& fall of sternum
mountains valleys or

the city bovine
leaning on one hoof

unbalanced but when ribs
return & sink

at least a tripod
stands or better still

four hooves in hope
of earthen stamp

if the pack drums
wake up chants

& if their dream-
fangs blunt or

if the last star
drones if the sky

is kids if I left
her gate a zoetrope

& hazy hours later
if the sal shine

silver over dogs
through fronds

through riper
breadfruit

no puff of smoke, no
charred wood, not even

cold ash—a bell
bigger than sky,

the plane, a simple
jet, & this morning

how a sweet
banana

gets inside, not just there
not just two, um, be specific
oh a vase of roses yellow
petals crystal stem but
not just, um, hesitation
out the window pointing
open palmed it's not be-
side it's not outside or even
even stomach swollen even
here & here it shows itself
specific sunlight slanting
through a thinner leaf

on the crown of the head
above the antlers, or flung

enameled on the floor, on
the sharpest wrist

on the ropes, the longer pools,
boulders strewn & roiling

roots blackened as if burnt
from wet, a constant humming

humming through the fontanel
& rushing stream, through

birch, through the graveled
split of standing deadwood

said I'm not so
into red

it warms the shoot
rajasic, as if

possible to quit
the scents of small

precision, scents
of buds pull afternoon

toward us, say
crimson buds

in flight—hard
to argue petals

higher up &
sometimes if you

do not look
you

tapioca butterfly
keeps the mountain

right, as if walking
kora, condors

wheeling cliffs, turning
the sky—aerial

prayer wheels, chevrons
under wing a soaring

glide of white above
the rhododendron forest

blooms too big to speak
& snowfields spill

in sympathy
with cumulous

holding our eyes wide
open to fog it cuts

the capstone back unheard
& ready for that glade

where kneecaps cleave
each cluster, cut

& paste in sympathy
with ground & pores—

the *covered* equal to
releasing cheekbones

press your forehead
to this golden

stump, flags
curl slowly round

in winter warmth
& gently now

there is no who to call,
you're faraway

a Hindi love song,
singing

pierces guts, rustles
trouser hems, they

catch the carpet—poke
your finger through

a brassy gong or
all the breakfast tea-

spoons tinkle piercing
whom among them

ranging over tree-line
spurting for an instant

juts up snow, facial still
our gathered muscles

trekking down, down the bridge
leans deeper into torrent

lower too we shinny over
paddies, then lakes

submerge us in our strength
of tones the brightest

outlines closer to the lakeshore
hulled by silt & grass

fern a lonely thorn the thorn
leans firm against the wind

against that blowing, leaning
into song, a wren, her song

for years or sometimes
less—they sleep in holes

"called to his eternal
home," back

straight & eyelash
rolling humble, dropping

face—flushed by sharper
breath, lets loose

the roots of teeth—
a field

fills worlds, the world
enameled and/or biting

east of me says rhythm
opens each one follows

on the next, towards
that east with features

bark in the brain, else-
where east of sirus

near a branch or skin—
the weight of them awake

at twilight still including
intimations & the mud

onto the allover friend
she feels as heat

it sucks at mud the sky
stills boughs of pine

bark now cool to palm
a wisp on the valley's

wall scatters green fern-
wet legs we ford

the falls knee-deep
in grey the flow

humps hidden rocks
& is it tuesday?

a book is just a book, but
such a book, so like a book

the jar is just a jar, the plates
sit dirty by the sink.

"if you have that book, that jar
those plates," he said, "I

will give them to you, but
if you don't, I'll take them back"

hand slides down
her belly dropping

down to swing in space
& how this equals

people—people
grow smaller &

they want & want
as much as each—some

grow very happy now
but stay asleep

heaps of pine a burnt out
cistern left abandoned &

the woodpile leaning—it will lean
again tomorrow, tongues

of dogs lie sprawling in the
dust, when sprawling

all directions even Buddha
isn't speaking, isn't

left abandoned for a stack
of sutras & a moldy *penguin-*

poets from the only
shop in town, it leans

arms spread dumb
to fuller reach her
leaf eyes sum her hair

blown over teeth across
her lips we call them that

collecting shifts with full
momentum & affection is
a package too returning

walnut shoulder rolled
& warming in the sun

nods her face & smiles
sometimes when I say how
sky is sometimes green remains

nearby, clear as palate
grasping liquid,
grasping at heat

sacrum is an atlas
simply softened, stacking
parts of fleshy surface

tied to a saved-up force,
sternum marked
for freedom—teaching

roots, seen instead of
terms gripping leaves,
see them spill

aorta softens brain
of sorts, shunted

in the posture not alone
the creature pads,

the big picture gone
from terms to spine

& kids throw sticks
through clouds, but clouds

just blow through sticks &
I no longer care

for books or even thoughts
of wood in a song

in this song in a dream
of rivers, what rivers?

how stories stagger as the stone
clouds overhead on autumn evenings
churn, until the back-brain floors
& the rain of hills lies down as hope
in cold ravines, in answers nearly
stained by evening. sometimes juniper
droops, juniper droops & the bridge
washed out by monsoon rush, spanned
by the rain-slick sheen of a log
underfoot, then only monsoon log, only
log—bodhi hung with clouds
closed to higher peaks, invisible
we wash among the stumps & milky
puddles, high strung ribs of cow & dung

when you get to the top
you bear right past
ruined walls & hay
bales molder wet
the brambles shriveled
now they're finished under
tattered sky leads up
to crags a wheat-cut
wisp of hair a toe or
pang of foot prolonged
to heel in clear & calming
waters rest releasing
plans beside some self
it's gone & better cool
stays now, so we stay
among the waters
& our own two feet
press mud gone autumn
mind behind the arch
belongs too right

the more you think on this,
holding & throwing

equals work—leaves rattle
in wind, a distant siren

hums lower than ears, at least
it seemed, for a moment

& it now seems...the more
you think, who hears?

sitting not just breathing
loosens ears.

when we heard about rain
we knew rain—not just

swell, but the middle-
way splash of river

curving means from thought
& soaking that trunk

flushes hidden
innocence—nerves

pulse at maps & stem
a tint towards

warmer cavities.
we pulse away

as creatures bloom, yes,
speak to all,

their lowering throats,
they loosen the roots

of their tongue,
together they hear

of families, friends
in bloom & pure

as a rose, no
question

calms a level sternum
where you're given
slow direction, truly

nesting in our yard,
nesting not for pretense
but for chest, & if

your ribs extend
the nest remains,
if not you tumble

I guess that means
we are a noisy place.
my hand remains a palm,

it sings from flowers spoons &
even from a picture frame—
that's nothing much,

I hear them pass &
in among the traffic sounds
the robins sing like walls

scooped up shit bare-
handed by a girl

the buffaloes organic
used by Genghis Khan

a tulsi bush still pruned
for balm, every leaf

returns to slo-mo
minaret & moldy tank

the steps leak blackened
water strings of moss &

cows chew peels or
fruit rinds plastic bag

listens for a twig switch broom
brushing limestone or an almond or
an architrave's nostalgic rose

& kneels inside the petalled shadow
while the swell of algae
darkens rusty grills

left it too long
for clouds

now turning, turning
round my feet—

they lengthen sharp
& seep towards

the back of the back-
brain, as rainfall

after rainfall
reveals sand

in the rice, thorns
in the mud

ensures the ease of torso's rise
to nothing, turned in every
sinew every socket filling

palm & doubled sole, our looking
pools & spreads specific e.g.
quiet gland & softened tongue

keep it clear towards us
stomach round & leafy things

sitting with a moment's
notice we recede to skin

faces linking to that voice,
a trace along the inner ear

the current runs when evening fronds
decay & cradled pine rise up

& up Orion's belt above
fresh panther kill—not grey

but bright & scrubbing
hard at the village pump

steaming stones, ready
for the torso, for dirt & duff,
for slow releasing eardrums,
soaking pores & mango
roots—the cattle's skinny
hips & hooves cut sharp
through moss as tattered vines
drip loose on flower tops
for saddhus, honey thick
in monsoon cloud

why we turn our torsos
backwards onto clouds of

winter, touch
on each the evening lengthens

feel the stretch towards
another space a situation

grounds the fingers cupped
on wood, white & glowing

friend of mercy. landscape
pardons hues for winter

trunk above the wrist observing
windows caught so many

clear the extra space
called lichen at the crest

need was cooler than a shout
for drifting anchored loosely

pulling here & there
the monkey tides lap up

against the sun-bleached
logs, how they come & go—

what anchor but a yellow petal
gust of wind or even

in the sedge a yarn
of something big

so others speak
of elsewhere as a noting

set apart enclosing me,
it pours to cleaner thought

& maybe from that shape
I sense a flight against

the lake from where the edge
supports a map & holds

the pouring out of every
other off that edge perhaps

in sympathy with landscape
loose in rain not leaking

you grip your fact
as a plunging

to whenever all
your sinews stretch &

bones thicken dense
whenever mental

boxes—lungs a giant
view of heaviness

closer to a moment
of your time please

churning breath, their own
increasing platform

twists increasing past
the jack pine

rooted, scratching into
hands, into your grip

so what is the world a valley—
slips into lightening, pours
away towards the lowered clouds

the only heir of the rain &
so are you such thunder
showers through your veins, on

this muddy slope a slip
trail washed by ash, soak
the gully's throat

reflections working
or the trunk still watching

all its own rotations—
why it's turning, arching

echoes, hum
an ear or wave,

my voice *hello*
to stones by stone

maybe your figure
feels escape, a flight

to where your wall
supports a roof—

maybe occupied
with huts, hiding

out from every re-
bound, maybe door?

snowflakes turn the bush
an almost phantom smoke

against that nebulae the blacker
space too cold to call it glade or even

how it weighs in the pines,
in the pines

hue & strength remembers
moss a lumber pile or
slash or shavings granite
shield together we remember
it's all flat they rest &
wonder all along the blossoms
& we rest too on the granite
hear the deodars surrounding
how they smell the shifting
dirt & outside landscape
in the calm of sleep I give
whatever once was space
the time clears timber stacks
repeats beside the road
we're full in our skin it's all
stretching not foreign no
I cut them in by holding wet
holding our legs tuned &
mending clear crags

barefoot women
bending old &

rigid in the dirt,
their dusty bangles

clink as they twitch
the dust & rubbish

into heaps of burning
tar, the road

itself now catches
fire burning mud

those little bits
of burning mud

for food & mud
for sleep it crackles

a flat stone
grazed by sunlight

boulders shining, alpine
mauve &

who it is
who doesn't know

repeating mauve
& mauve

protects her mind,
gone—what's gone

or better (better?) still
what isn't?

hear if numbers or weights
might lower your eardrums, hear

if any might act but
taste the autumn falling

still your value arches
over sounds, the waves

might offer space or mind
as trunk, as voice *hey you*

might strip the bones if bone
might throw them up to hold

skin a vine the steady plain
a night stretched to small
still tanks & smaller quartz
of healthy skin a vine

near a roof where the door
creaks low from a gust
removing every thought—

a vine removing, how it
loosens everyone the wind
& how through leaves

no glimpse of rocks
or stones & then

no glimpse, no
rocks, not even

stones—what
is a glimpse &

is it clear and/
or rocky? what about

the distant cliff
here in this room?

flooded puddle empties
to a brook, it leaks

the ball of your foot now long
to the heel in the clear

white waters releasing
the plot beside

someone else gone &
simple anyhow

aims his telling at the real
arising from that hole

aware of lower pools,
the hearth a warming

muck & salty dhal
blackening the pot

smeared with ghee at the tin
plate's edge, Chinese

music powered
by an old car cell—no

cars here, 10 K
from Tibet (hundreds

by footpath).
cleats at rest

in someone's eyes, rest
up north if ever green

& salty fern
caught paw

cones & cliffs fade upwards
into rain-clouds. a milky stream
runs down the mountain

turning it to foxes, combed
by their scent, until ending
charts beyond. watch

if planned by legs, by feet.
we lean so close to clear
this bark, this peeling back
an engine made from pith

at places yes all places
clear reflections

working added or the spine
observing revolution

which is why it loops
so well along so frayed,

over left & me still drinking
mountain fruit, drunk

I sit no bigger—
not who lived an old

old man but how he hesitates
& hesitates to lend a clearer

perch or maybe angle
of your skin towards

that four-foot pressure.
ok magpie stretching out

the nerve the squirrel & badger
& your hand spread hers

the past remains diverted
to a drone which gives

awareness to the turning
exhalation over acres

& then depth if there's lift,
lifting too clearly

from practice so simple,
so *about* & also each:

us & space in London too
& even in a smaller meal

in every raising
flanks of light

your practice slides
entwined with tools

flesh on the floor
trying to flatten

& spread it all
remaining vapor

"your work makes no
sense" she laughed

stopping so bright so
poor but then they snap

so often every bit
by bit & every

nasturtium blooms the same
a sunken garden foothills dry

& hot above a measured reading
Keats' "philosophy will clip

an angel's wings" the spread out
shin for shank & foot for groin

I mean the ball of the foot
or me for you organic &

a word for us the sun
for bread, palm to the small

of your back & walnut skin
for summer twilight

turns & air returns
the leaves still green

above your ears
those brainwaves rolling,

it's a fact and I listen
to the big-deal story, sure

you wash your bowl you
rake the leaves